TIGERHEART

The Poet

Written, Art, and Pictures by

Mike Stevenson Fleury

1st Books rev. 04/26/01

TIGERHEART

THE POET

MIKE STEVENSON FLEURY

Illustrations by Mike Stevenson Fleury

CONTENTS

Introduction

Although Mike Stevenson Fleury has two poems published on the Internet and in two poetry books, and is currently working on his biography, this is the first book he has ever published. Tigerheart is a nicknamed which he got from martial arts school. He was born on October 13, 1973. His father is French Canadian, but his mother was born in Haiti.

Mike had gone through a lot as a child. Unfortunately, his parents had grown apart because his mother had always been independent, therefore, never had time for anybody else. As a result, he and his father grew very close until his mother came back with a lie, and convinced his father to let her son see her family in Haiti for his ninth birthday. That was the last time he saw his father. As a result, Mike had found himself hidden and isolated from his father at a boarding school in Haiti.

Years later, his mother did come back for him. On July 8th, 1988, she flew him to come live with her in Brooklyn, NY. As a multilingual, multi-talented, and a quick learner, he fell in love with many things. He was writing poetry, and acting in plays he wrote himself back in John Dewey High School, which he graduated from in June of 1993. It wasn't until January of 1995 when he finally made up his mind about which college he wanted to attend because he enjoys doing too many things. So with the help of a close high school friend she convinced him to come pick up a brochure with her at the college she wanted to attend. (Long Island University, located at 1 University Plaza, in Brooklyn.)

There, he majored in Media Arts which is consisted of Photography, Film and Video Productions, News Writing and TV Productions, Computer Graphics, and many other media related courses. Also he minored in Speech and Theater to control his shyness and stage fright since he also had a passion for acting on stage and in front of the camera. Despite all his accomplishments at LIU, such as writing, producing, directing, editing . . . and playing the main role in his own movie named, "Tigerheart, the Untypical Biker," he joins clubs such as Sound and LIU-TV where he videotaped and photographed many on and off-campus events like gospel groups and basketball games, he never completed his degree. Out of the 128 credits his degree required, he needed about 9 credits to graduate. However, he attempted to take the remaining courses in summer of 1999, but they only offered one of the courses. Confused and frustrated, he ran off and got his commercial driver's license where he got several jobs driving tractor-trailers, buses, trucks, and for a school bus company.

As a matter of fact he wrote most of these poems while driving, and on the job. He plans on returning for his college degree once he has his first child which he desperately needs with the right girl which he's been searching for. Finally he guarantees these poems to educate, entertain, as well as motivate the reader.

LOVE, AS IT COMES & GOES

Since the beginning of life
Lots of love has been shared.
Although invisible and non-physical
It comes in so many mysterious ways.
Of all our compelling emotions
Love's the most vital and fascinating one.
The joy and happiness that come with love
Always seem to be the most important in our daily lives.
The hard-breathing and sensation which take over one's body
Are quite magical.
Those that have already been in love will always agree
That a heart that hasn't felt love is an empty one.
A body that hasn't been caressed and embraced by love
Will die a terribly sad and lonely death
Where its unrested soul will continue to wonder up above
Seeking to express and share all the inner magic
Which the whole love package
Fills everyone's heart with since day one.
I can still feel the love current
Running out of control through my desperate veins.
I can't endure it much longer.
It's gradually taking me apart.
I'm so thirsted for love.
I need to be touched.
I want to feel humanly alive.
Please! Please! Please!

Mike Stevenson Fleury

CIVILIZED

What does civilize really mean?
Do we live up to its definition?
What would the animals say if they could talk?
Would they think we're really civilized?
Or would they say we're just fooling ourselves?
We really need to question ourselves.

At times I can almost feel the animals pointing and laughing at me.
Well, why wouldn't they?
They may not speak our language
But they're not blind and stupid.
They sure are silently observing our bad deeds.

Although they are shocked and furious by them
Unfortunately they can't offer us their bright opinions.
They laugh at us when we hurt our brothers.
They point at us when we let greed control us.
They try harder to teach us how to really live.
We instead follow our own directions.

When I look at nature I often wonder who's really running it.
But I know for sure that we're destroying it.
Could the cavemen had been right all along?
That, we may never know for sure
Since to us,
We are CIVILIZED.

I AM

Like a dead kitten I lie on this cold pavement.
Nights and days pass me by.
I am dead.
But again, I'm alive
For I see and feel it all.

As people walk by and stare.
As cars run over my long intestine
Stretching from my tail to the sidewalk.
I am sadden
By these kids who know no better.

Running their bikes repeatedly over my head.
I've been stared, ignored, and abused.
But my soul still lives.
For they don't care to bury my small body.
Rather, I get spit on and stepped on.
Like a poor orphan I cry for a mother.
Like a dry rose in the burning sun I starved for water.
But luckily, I feel snow flakes falling on me.
Maybe they will bury me completely.
Or perhaps lead me down to the sewer below me.

Mike Stevenson Fleury

CRYING OUT

Suffering is everywhere
But help is nowhere.
Racists are striking
But nobody's protecting.
Let us cry out!

Hatred is causing destruction
But there seems to be no solution.
Nature's erosions show up stronger
But no one realizes that it is God's anger.
When will we . . . for crying out louder?

I often sit in a quiet corner
Wondering whether one man can make a difference.
Day after day, I see more homelessness and world hunger.
Obviously, it might take more than one man's conscience.
Luckily, I smell help coming closer.

ANGEL

Like a lost angel
She lands by my tree.
Like a miracle,
Again she's free.
I've searched every angle
And finally she's here.

Like lightning on this Wednesday,
I am struck by her beauty.
For this rainy day
Will forever be pretty
For it is the day
When I met my sweetie.

On her lips, I see smiling the morning sun.
But in her eyes, cries the rain of dawn.
Smile my love, smile
For your sweetness won't be in vain.
Shine my love, shine
As your soul mate glows in the rain.

Mike Stevenson Fleury

THE SUN

Every single day
I observe it rising up the sky.
Never misses a day of its chores.
Sometimes,
I see when it's sad in the early morning.
Its sadness usually leads to tears.
Although we show no sympathy.
We use its tears rather to drink and bathe.
Fortunately and unexpectedly,
It gets very angry.
In the process,
We feel the HEAT of its anger,
The PAIN of its fire,
And the sweat of its resistance.
Why is it as angry?
To it,
It's as obvious as it is
To us.

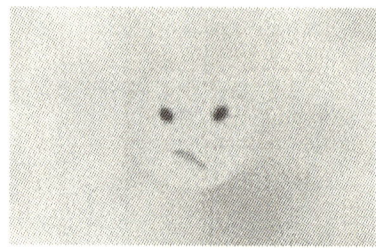

ISOLATED DARKNESS

Unbearably sitting
In my dark place.
Although in a continuous darkness
I wait
For a miracle to strike.
From here I see the light,
Bright as the moon.
Unfortunately, it cannot reach my spot.
CRICKETS
Singing their loud melodies,
Just to keep me away.
COURAGE
They give me instead.
AND LUCKY I AM,
To hear a very close sound of the ocean.
WAVES fight the strongest wind
IN MY ADVANTAGE IT IS.
Again water splashes and reaches my face
THIRSTY I'LL NEVER BE.
Nevertheless,
I shall never be fully satisfied
Till the world overcomes,
LIGHTS MY WAY OUT,
But never,
Never the color of my skin.

Mike Stevenson Fleury

UNUSUAL DREAM

One afternoon,
An old man I saw
Walking along with his wooden chair by his side.
In front of him stood the biggest mountain I ever saw.
Amazingly, somehow he managed to climb to the top.
He could be seen by everyone in the village.

Way up there, he stood staring at the clouds motionless.
Moments later, a sudden rainy storm breaks out around the mountain.
As cautious and confused we all were, we proceeded for a closer look.
As lightning flares start aiming , my followers retreated.
But I ducked and hid behind a huge stone.

Then I noticed a tornado forming in the sky.
Later it dropped and started to spin around the old man.
He never moved a muscle.
Suddenly it stood still before the ol' man.
And apparently both parties were having a conversation.

Soon after the tornado had vanished
The man began going up the sky
As if he were being pulled up by an invisible rope.
As I tried to climb up the mountain
A group of stones started sliding down in my direction.
So I quickly got the message.

Running back to the village, I turned for a last look
But the man was nowhere in sight.
And then I woke up.
But to this day, I foresee myself on that same mountain.
It may not be in a dream,
But I have to leave it up to God to decide.

COLORS

I love colorful things.
From animals to human beings.
I look in the sky
And see colorful birds.
We are surrounded by beautiful colors.

Naturally, nature is made of colors.
There behind the mountain is a huge rainbow,
Bright and colorful.
This is beautiful!
It's what nature tries desperately to teach us.

I want to spread my seeds
For I love my colorful world.
I want to exchange my seeds
With different colors of girls
For I love a colorful world.

There behind the mountain are also two horses.
A black stallion and a white female horse
Experiencing their gift of love,
As they cherish their colors and ignore others' ignorance
Yes, they do understand!
But will we ever?

Mike Stevenson Fleury

YOU'RE ON MY MIND

Since the first time I saw you
Wherever I go
I can always feel your presence.
Whatever I do it's you that I see
Although it's just an illusion.

Every time I close my eyes
Trying to dream of you
As though you're nuts about me too
Lights from your sparkling eyes
Shine my face as they're fixed on mine.

Unfortunately, there's one obstacle in the way.
What can I do to win your poor virgin heart, my angel?
Without it, I'm like a wet flower in constant darkness,
A stomach without food,
Or a pen without ink.

I can't bear it to see you in pain as well.
It kills me even more inside.
My heart isn't as empty since you exist in mine
However, yours is, for I am missing in yours.
I'm trying my best to reach you sweetie.

If I could rescue your heart
I would lock it next to mine
Where it can never be harmed.
Please hand me your heart so I may show you the way
Right onto this forgotten world.

Here we both can cherish this peaceful garden of love
Where there's plenty of fresh air, roses, and everlasting love.
A garden specially made for love birds.
For once, we both can join them in collecting twigs
To create our own nest of love.

TIME VS. DISASTER

It's a quarter to 2:00 a.m.
Still I cannot fall asleep.
I'm lying in my bed by my window
Observing the scariest storm ever.
It frightens me.

It's now exactly 3:00 a.m.
I cut the light off and the annoying radio.
Here I am closing my eyes, hoping to go explore a wonderful dream.
Oh-oh, I cannot . . . I'm really scared.
There's a nightmare outside.

It's a minute to 3:15 a.m.
I roll over facing the window again
With the sheet over my head.
Suddenly something bangs at my window.
Scary but I manage for a glimpse of the scene.

Hey, outside is quite empty.
It's just the wind and the trees
Dancing together from left to right.
The wind and trees are finally giving me a break.
But as the trees keep falling down, it touches me deeply.

The trees are all covered with mud
While a flood of dirty water washes everything in his path.
Poor helpless creatures struggle to stay alive.
Looks like they're losing this battle.
The rain, the wind, and this dreadful darkness are my awakened nightmare.

Mike Stevenson Fleury

LOST IN THE DARK

As life goes on
Love goes by.
Naturally, love takes us all
To complex journeys.
Often to everlasting peace of mind and tender.
As I crawl in tears in the dark
I feel completely empty and lonely Since love
Has yet to discover me.

At times I use this warm sand which nature offers me
To repose my exhausted and impractical body
Where I often dream of ever seeing daylight again.
But the cries of the seabirds and this silent obscurity
Are all which I'm surrounded by.
I need an escape.
Here, when I think of my hardship
I just cry my way to sleep
For life sure has its mysterious ways of punishing a love-seeker.
But what have I done to deserve this?
What have I done to get shut out in this manner?
The tranquility of this long lasting night is quite sublime.
This poor corporal frame of mine
Struggles to bear this frightening mood.
I wonder how long it will endure this sad perplexity
While it stands here,
lacking the vital and soothing attentions.
I know and have heard of love
Where two people can create remarkable magic together.
Yet my body has been stripped of most of its emotions.
From here, I can hear lovers mooching around.
For nature to have secluded me very far away
From all forms of passion,
Obviously, I may never, ever feel love again.
I also know of beauty when it stands before me
But this darkness also controls that.
For all the sweet sounds and harmonies I sense
Of tender joy with warmer and purer love I want
I sure am lost forever.

THE BIG VISION

I envision my death.
It was in a dream.
Set in the future.
It was on my birthday in the year 2065.

For I saw a soundless train,
Fast and comfortable,
With tracks connecting New York with New Jersey.
I was an old man
Riding on the train for the first time
When suddenly it happened.

Out of nowhere a huge flying ship
Come out of the clouds.
We all were stunned when it fired at us,
Knocking the entire train off its tracks.
And down we went
Plunging into the river.

I did not die right away.
For a long time I watched myself drowning.
My saddest moment ever.
I tried all the exits,
But there was no way out.
Such loneliness and hopelessness!

The train kept going down and down.
Down to the abyss.
I never felt it touching the bottom of the sea.
And suddenly came complete darkness and silence.
And I woke up.

Should I worry?
Why should I?
For I shall have lived a long healthy life
And died a painless death.
Isn't that everyone's death wish?

13

Mike Stevenson Fleury

I'M WAITING

Waiting for my baby to be born.
I listen to it swim
Everyday and every night
When I rest my ear gently
Upon the mother's big belly.
Is it responding to me?
What is this sweet voice I hear
Telling me to be patient?
But how can I
When I keep dreaming of you
Everyday and every night.
Wow!
Watching these bulgy eyes fixed upon mine,
As my baby crawls out,
Eager to greet me with the first smile
Before blessing me with the sweet cry
Oh, how I hold my baby
Against my chest!
Refusing to let go.
How the resemblance
Sparkles upon our faces!
Oh I felt so reborn,
Joyful and alive!
I refuse to wake up
Into my real world
Where I will struggle to wait
Till this dream comes alive
Where it will surely last a lifetime
In my physical world.

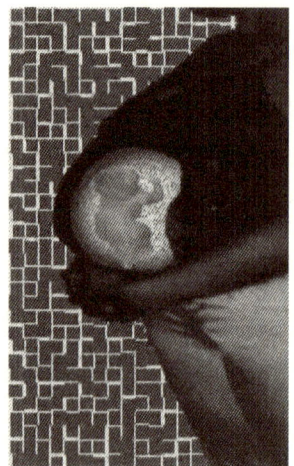

14

THE TRUCKER

I'm a trucker.
I live to drive
And drive to live.
I was born with sight
But all I see is
Rain and snow,
Sunrise and sunset,
Mile markers and exits,
Other drivers and dead animals,
Passing me as I head for this distant and lonely horizon
Which becomes blurry when I feel tired.
I should rest my body now tells me.
First let me drive upon a safe truck stop.
Here we go!
Hey, who's that disturbing my beauty sleep?
It's only a hooker trying to make a living.
Sorry I can't be a client.
I have a family back in New York.
I do miss them painfully.
Missed them for the past four years I've been on the road.
Sure wish I could have taken them along.
Maybe the wife will understand.
Will my kids ever?
I feel like a loner.
A deadbeat dad.
But I'm neither.
I'm only a trucker
Picking this way to make a living
One mile at a time.

Mike Stevenson Fleury

LIFE

Life is a mystery,
A challenge,
As well as a puzzle.
Those that understand it
Or those that know its value
Live a meaningful long life.
But those that make the wrong choices
Live a short worthless life.
Life tests every living thing
And it rarely gives second chances.
I observe and learn.
I follow its rules
And I'm still living.

THE OFFICER

I'm a white cop.
I feel invisible.
I own a gun and plenty of bullets.
I get to pick who deserves a bullet.
I own some cuffs,
A big baton and plenty of mace.
I am God!
I get to wear two different uniforms.
A white one and a dark one.
I enjoy both of my professions
Although I only get paid for one.
I play a cop during the day
And a KKK member at night.
I don't just burn crosses.
I harass anything that's nonwhite
And harm anything that's black.
Young or old,
Male or female,
It doesn't matter to me
For I own this country.
Black will never be my favorite color.
I'm the perfect disguise.
So let the silent war continue.

Mike Stevenson Fleury

LOST IN BROOKLYN

Growing up in the Bronx
I've seen it all.
From drug dealers to gang violence.
Coming from girlfriend's place
I make a wrong turn
And I find myself in Brooklyn.
The wrong place to be on a rainy night.
Watching all those eyes fixed on me,
I sense they know I'm lost.
They know I'm a stranger.
As I check my environment
All the territories are marked and claimed.
I look at those vicious eyes.
They tell me to exit my car.
I will,
Over my dead body.
I shall remain in here
For those eyes aren't friendly at all.
If I shall die in Brooklyn tonight
It shall be in my car
For outside is wet and filled with hungry wolves.
Angel, if you do exist
I need your help now
For I am too young to die.
I'm only 17.

THE BIKER

I'm a biker.
An untypical biker.
One with special needs and feelings.
I cry for a son!
A piece of my soul.
I live on the fast lane.
I seek a replacement,
But the thrill is all worth it
For the rush is fulfilling.
It's never about the mud
Which my tires spray on pedestrians,
How fast I get from the park to the beach,
The noise which shakes the entire neighborhood,
The trails of dust and smoke I leave behind,
Nor the honeys I take for a ride.
It's way more personal.
I cry for a son!
It's been years of desperation
And months of false hopes.
Can't afford to stop crying
For I'm getting old
And it is my destiny.
Son, I picture us on the road
Riding on my set of wheels,
As we dress alike.
Like father and son.
Oh, I cry for a son!
I shall keep crying
For hopefully he shall hear my cry.

Mike Stevenson Fleury

THE BIG HIT

I hit the jackpot.
Zeros run across the whole check.
Yet I'm happy.
I can now kiss misery goodbye.
I got the break I needed
And the chance I so long awaited.
The chance to help the less fortunate.
The journey has started!
It's time to ensure that suffering's abolished.
Whether it's hunger or homelessness,
Everyone deserves happiness
Before he or she is terminated
For I am smarter than other rich men.
For I do not believe in greed but equality.
I do listen to God's requests
For he shall save me a greater reward way above.
Eternal life.

THE MARTIAL ARTIST

I'm a martial artist.
My fists and feet are my life
For They're been keeping me alive.
I never seek trouble.
I let it come to me.
For when it comes,
Like a raging flood
I make people fall in the mud.
Like an angry tiger
I do not control my anger.
I show no mercy
For they are not upstanding citizens
But merely bad guys who hurt others for fun.
I should feel no sorrow
For I was taught to defend myself.
Preventing some serious blows
From invading my body is only rational,
But as the tiger takes control
It shall return the blows back to its opponents.

LET THE BABY CRY

Let the baby cry
For it is her right.
Let the baby cry
For she can't yet talk.
Let the baby cry
But don't pick her up.
Let the baby cry
And she won't be a brat.
Let the baby cry
Or give her a bottle.
Let the baby cry
But don't you dare answer that door
For it is the Jehovah Witness people.

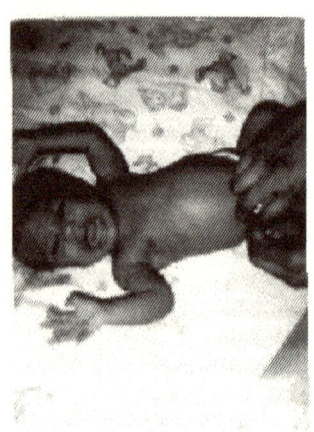

THE END

Dream or no dream
I'm happy
For the end has finally come.
Like a flock of birds migrating
The sky is crowded with people.
People of all ages and colors.
But they're not all heading to the same place.

Way above There are two planets waiting
A moon-like planet
And a sun-like planet.
Like lost balloons we float in the sky.
As I float in the sky
It's a shame to see only a few are heading to my planet
But I'm still glad to feel no heat where I'm heading.

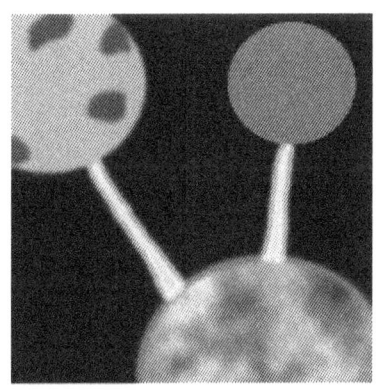

Mike Stevenson Fleury

THE DOOR

From a baby to an adult
I'm now a man.
Afraid to face up
For it is scary to leave home
For it still feels like yesterday
When I rode my tricycle in the backyard.
Have I been sleeping
For time to have passed me by so fast?
What ever happened to my childhood?

Like a hen tells her chicks
I've been told it's time.
But how do I learn to behave like a man?
It was never taught to me.
Which way should I head
When nothing is being handed to me now?

I have the job
But it pays low.
I can get the apartment
But it must be cheap.
How will I cope with this loneliness?
This horror I face!

I'll need a pet.
If not, a woman.
I'll need to be a parent
For every kid I see is a parent.
Am I late?
Oh, I'm jealous.
Will I make it?
Will I adjust?
Will I survive?
Will I be homeless?
Only time will tell.

TOUGH DECISION

It is five p.m..
And I grew up in the projects.
Here I am again standing
On the edge on the projects'
Tallest building.

As I stand here trembling
I try to make the toughest decision of my short life.
Should I keep hiding?
Or should I end my pathetic life
By leaping?

But which death is less painful?
Maybe a bullet from these drug dealers down below?
It's just too painful
To watch people below,
People running and kids ducking
As though they were trained to react as such.

For these senseless wars of brothers against brothers
Are definitely a waste of mankind.
For these innocent kids and bystanders
Ought to be living their lives to the fullest.
Such violence must be put to rest
For my time is up.

Watching repeatedly these nightmares
Where authorities won't step up
Against these dream stealers.
While the death rate is up
If I step up I sure won't come out alive
So I shall take my final step out of this war zone.

Mike Stevenson Fleury

SHATTERED DREAMS

I'm a 13-year-old girl with a baby.
My innocence wasn't completely taken away from me.
I gave it away
In exchange for love and attention.
My boyfriend didn't know any better,
And we sure didn't want any baby.
We were two stupid kids who thought sex was love.
Unlike my 15-year-old sister
My innocence wasn't robbed by a grown man.
The government provides her and baby with a safe haven.
WELFARE, meaning,
Without Education Life For Anyone Remains Experimental.
And many girls today lure themselves into such lifestyle.
For I cannot be a full-time mother and a full-time student.
As far as my boyfriend
I'm placing an "Ex" before that word
For he has run to his mother denying our baby.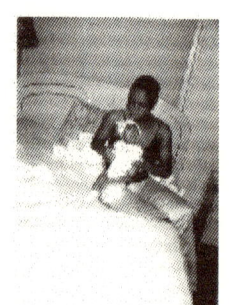
And now I'm an uneducated single mother.
I don't blame him though
But those in power
For how can a frightened boy be a father?
Can't correct my mistakes now
But I can preach to other kids.
Those in power can't prevent ten sex
But they can prevent teen pregnancy.
Some kind of tough love must be enforced
For with 911, parents cannot discipline their children.
As a result we have out of control kids.
This is serious business
For I watch daily TV talk shows.
I predict the fall of this country
For a bunch of dropout single parents cannot be leaders.
Well it is the American way.
Problems aren't looked into until it is too late.
With this kind of attitude
Problems will keep piling up
For this country lacks significant leaders and great thinkers.

26

BROKEN HEART

Lying peacefully by my window as I stare at those trees
I can feel the love and support which they're silently offering me.
This great joy I feel watching the leaves waving at me
As each branch gradually swings constantly from left to right.

They sure seem very happy dancing in this cool breeze
As the wind gently blows in their wonderful green ears.
This beautiful scene surely takes my breath away.
As well as my mind away from all my sadness and sorrow.

I now feel the pain gradually settling down as the tears fade away.
I have to go on with my life the leaves tell me.
Now I know that every time I see her lovely face before me
Or whenever I keep hearing her sweet voice caressing my ear
That she'll always find me by my bedroom window

Chatting with my new green quiet folks
Where I will always manage to cope
With al the anguish and loneliness she's caused me
After having broken my poor virgin heart.
Dumping me so harshly and severely.
But as my new friends tell me, 'the world must keep turning.'

Mike Stevenson Fleury

CONFUSED

I'm a man with many dreams.
Also a man with many talents.
I'm thankful for having been blessed with these talents.
However, problem is
I cannot decide which one to put to use.
I feel like I'm chained in a steel cage.
This isolation I feel
Has brought me so much confusion.
Should I go ahead and become a poet?
How 'bout an author?
Hey, I write good songs too.
So maybe just a song writer?
How 'bout a singer?
But I love acting!
I also love driving tractor-trailers for a living.
See what I mean?
So much confusion!

28

SUMMER TIME

Summer.
The best season of all.
Summer time,
A time to get out,
Seeking fun on the beach
While enjoying the great sights
Of females running on the shore in sexy bikinis.

Summer.
The hottest season ever.
A time to walk your dog
Or walk with your lover in the park.
A time to roll on the grass
As you passionately kiss your lover.

Summer time.
A time to sit in your backyard with your lover
As you both enjoy some Bar-B-Q.
It is a time to take the whole family out
To watch the hottest movies.
Oh my summer time!
A time for great ideas.

Mike Stevenson Fleury

WINTER

Winter.
A pretty, deadly season.
For it is a time for all kinds of accidents.
The best of winter only comes on Christmas.
For it is the time when families gather up to exchange love and gifts.

In winter time,
I still prefer staying indoors.
Before exchanging gifts I usually stay in bed
Making love to my lover.

Like two caterpillars we cuddle,
Enjoying the heat of our passion
And the sweat of our love
As we both squeeze all the love sensation out
While watching snow flakes
Hitting our windows
And the birds dancing in the falling skies.

SPRING

Spring.
The quiet rainy season.
The season of rebirth.
Everything that dies in the Fall,
Comes back to life in the Spring.
From dry flowers to leafless trees.

Spring is also a time for new beginnings.
A time to start over.
A time for second chances.
Therefore, a time to change your old habits.
A time to forgive your friends and those closer to you.
A time to watch your kids and friends play outside
As you sadly sit on the porch.

Sadly staring at small creatures
Playing in the trees
And others making love in the grass.
For they tell us to think as others as brothers
And to reach out to the less fortunate
For they deserve respect, love, food, and shelters like you.

Mike Stevenson Fleury

GIRL POWER

The power of a woman is unlike many powers.
She is known as the weaker sex,
Whereas men as the strongest sex.

To a woman, our strength only comes handy
When she needs help with heavy things
To her,
We are brainless
And still haven't evolved completely from the cavemen.
She thinks that she's very much in control of her destiny.

It's like money.
She makes the world go around.
She's the true survivor.
Her body is her fortune
And her mind is her temple.
We'd rather die than paying her no attention.

Walking on the streets in her sexy outfit,
All eyes must turn on her.
And I do mean all eyes
For everyone feels the power.
A power,
Strong enough to make other women look.

Whether these women look for different reason than men's
They still find the time to turn their heads and look.
Therefore, her power is felt by both sexes.
For a girl to possess such power
She ought to be respected
And observed with a third eye.

NATURAL WOMAN

I love my natural woman.
My natural woman wears no weave
For an accident won't take place.
She wears no make up
For it may rain.
She wears no pushup bras
So she feels no pain.
She wears no wig
For it is windy outside.
She wears no glasses
For she won't be called four eyes.
She gets no butt-implant
For it is never wise.

Mike Stevenson Fleury

THE KING

I'm a lion.
A very rational lion.
Humans call me king of the jungle.
It cannot be because I live off dead flesh.
Perhaps it's due to the fear they have for me.
For dead-flesh eating isn't just practiced by me.
Even humans feed off dead flesh.

But I puke on humans.
They disgust me
For I never kill in vain.
Only to feed my family and me.
I have no need for violence.
But why do humans solve their conflicts with violence?

That is quite irrational.
To let one's self be controlled by greed is not responsible.
For when humans die
We animals wonder why.
Why all the violence on their own kind
When all the possessions will be left behind?

THE STRANGER

Being from out of town
Can be hazardous to your health.
Especially if you cannot defend yourself.
One weekend I drove from upstate to Long Island
Where I quickly made a few friends.

They all had one thing in common.
A red bandana.
I thought they looked cool in them.
So I asked for an extra bandana.

I thought it was nice of them
Not charging me for it.
All I had to do was fight them
And they'd let me have it.

Again, being out of town
Can be hazardous to your health.
For when I realized I was to be the bait
It was already too late.
As they moaned and groaned on the
ground
All I heard was, 'no deal! You go buy your own.'
But I had to seize me a red bandana.

Mike Stevenson Fleury

FAITH

I try desperately to believe
But bad things keep happening to me.
I try believing in destiny
But is it my destiny to be so damn unlucky?

If there exists so-called destiny
I should then sit and do nothing in life
And destiny shall find me the right path in life.
But wouldn't I be waiting for eternity?

I even try believing in God
But why isn't everyone equal?
Why is there so much suffering,
So much greed and struggle
While the innocents are being crushed?

As God, I sure would put a cease to misery.
For God to be the sole creator of this planet,
The sun and the moon which we depend on,
How then he came about?
If he merely exists due to coincidences
So does the entire universe.

I wait desperately for an answer.
A concrete one by the creator himself.
Not by some preacher with an old text.
I heard God had spoken in the past.
Speaking again today couldn't have been a better time.
For it'd free my mind and make many believers today.

I see people doing very wrong things
And they're still living.
I choose to do the right things
And I'm still living.
I maybe wasting my time today
But I'd be furious discovering so tomorrow.

THE PERFECT FATHER

I'm 16 years old.
I don't know my father.
Therefore, he doesn't exist to me.
For all I have of him is a black and white picture.

The way I remember him kissed my mother a long time ago
Could have fooled any bright girl.
So it's not mother's fault for him to have shut me out of his life.
From day one he was simply a lowlife sperm donor in disguise.
My mother was too in love to have noticed it.

He's turned my life upside down.
Now I have no idea how to be a son
For I have no father to teach me how.
I'm scarred for life.

Mother has tried to play a father figure
But she can't heal a wounded heart.
She holds a bigger responsibility.
Being a mother to me.
A perfect father does not run from his family.
A perfect father takes care of his responsibility.
He works as a team with the mother.
He ensures that everything is taken care of.
A perfect father doesn't miss the birth of his son.
Nor his first smile, step, word, cry, laughter, and graduation.

Though a struggling mother
She still finds time to fill in as a father.
She checks my homework before putting me to sleep.
It's just too much for a single mother.
It's just not fair.

Mike Stevenson Fleury

THE PERFECT BEING

Her figure!
How it sticks on my mind!
The deep breath I take
Every time I think of her body.
The seduction!
The way she walks toward me.
The incredible sensation
She brings upon me
In the heat of passion.
How her touch opens every pore on my body!
How I rest my head on her bosom!
The joy I feel making love to her!
The magic we always create in bed!
The perspiration!
The close connection!
She makes me want to live forever.
For she is the perfect being.
The most amazing being.
Women!
How they are special!
Enough to carry another being
For nine months long
With it swimming and breathing,
Eating and kicking,
Sleeping and smiling
In their huge stretchable bellies.
For all the pain they go through
Pushing out a baby,
They deserve to be cherished and worshiped
For they'll always be the perfect being.

WISHES

I wish I were president
For I would resolve every incident.
I dream of a drug-free country.
I also dream of a racist-free country.

I dream of a productive society.
I also dream of a gun-free society.
I dream of a rape-free place.
I also dream of a friendly human race.
I dream of human compassion.
I also dream of a hate group-free nation.

What would your dreams be
If you were president?
For if I were president
I would resolve every incident

DO YOU FEEL ME

I see,
I feel,
And I write.

You read,
You feel,
And you wonder.

I use words,
You use your eyes,
And you learn.

I make the offer,
You take the advice,
And you live happily.

HAIKU No. 1

A bearded lady
What a scary sight
For she scared the living hell out of me.

HAIKU No. 2

*I'm a midget
I get bullied and stepped on
As though I'm not human.*

CAMPING

As a boy I used to go camping with my dad.
Now as a man I go camping alone.
Not a bright idea.
For I am so scared.
Here I am lying in this tent
On this rainy night.
I feel so secluded and lonely.
I can hear of kinds of sounds
Coming from creatures of the night.
Should I turn off my lantern?
Are the creatures headed for my small tent?
My cheap watch has stopped working.
And the night seems endless.
Will I ever come out of this jungle alive?
If I get killed here
I sure am lost forever.
I hope it's the wind shaking my tent.
If it is Big Foot or a curious bear
I am a dead man!
While I think of my last line
I pray for the sun to come to my rescue
For I am tired
Lying alone in this cold mud.

Mike Stevenson Fleury

I WANT TO CLAIM MY BABY

I want to claim my baby
But she's nowhere in sight
I shall not just let it be

Ooh I want to see her blow
As I'm flying my kite
I want to claim my baby

I will never let her go
Forever I'll be holding her tight
I shall not just let it be

Since I'm made of dough
She shall be mine tonight
I want to claim my baby
I shall not just it be.

WHAT IS IT?

In winter time
It can really be hard.
Hard enough to carry tons of weight.
And cold enough to freeze life out of living flesh.
In summer time
It's still very cold.
Also soft, quiet, wild, and unpredictable.
It can get angry and still has control over itself.
It is the most powerful force on earth.
We all rely on it to survive.
It is the reason for rainy days
Therefore, all life on earth.

LISTEN UP BABY!

I tried to be nice
Even took your damn dog for a walk
Said I tried to be nice
But I was taken for an exhausting jog
I think I'm so damn lucky to be alive
For he dragged my ass across a goddamned moving truck

Will you ever be mine baby?
Cause I ain't mad at your dog at all
I said will you ever be mine baby?
Cause I ain't mad at your dog at all
Trust me baby if I were
I woulda kicked your ugly dog ten thousand times

So honey what the hell's keeping you
From saying you want me just as much?
Baby what the hell's keeping you
From saying you want me just as much?
And I just really hate when you stare at your dog
When he's nailing another bitch

MINDING MY OWN MY BUSINESS

As I drive down
this filthy road

I look in the rear
view mirror to see what

angel is on my tail in
that red flashy corvette

she is smiling and waving
at me to tell me to pull

over I then got a clear view
of her huge melons

as they jiggle like
a fresh jell-o as
they make their way

toward me
forgive me if I start
thinking sexual thoughts

its not my fault at
all she's teasing me

Mike Stevenson Fleury

COMING OUT

I was born in the wrong world.
Or perhaps in the wrong century
For I have seen too many senseless hate crimes.
People are so judgmental.
They think they can tell others wrong from right.
Yet they are sinners themselves.

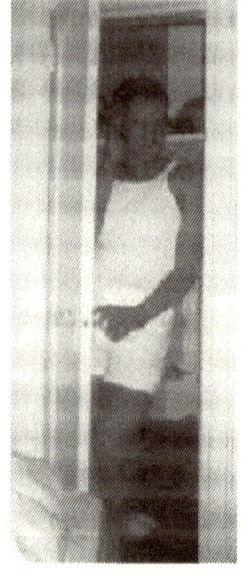

I'm quite aware of my obvious differences
Like I'm aware that every human is different.
We have short people
And we have tall people.
We have so-called while people
And we have so-called colored people.
We have so-called straight people
And we have so-called gay people.

I guess I belong to the gay category
For I don't make love to women.
I guess I belong to the gay category
For I sound feminine.
I guess I belong to the gay category
For I walk feminine.
I guess I belong to the gay category
For I fight like women.

If everyone would mind their own business
I wouldn't be writing these lines
For everyone would live in harmony.
I'm opening the door now.
I'm coming out!
Out of the closet
For I've got a life to live
Like everyone on this planet.

THE INMATE

I'm in prison.
How did I get here?
I just asked for a ride home.
Is this for real?
25 years to life?
Hell no!
For what?

Somebody's going down for this.
Starting with the damn judge.
Then the idiot cops who handcuffed me.
They made a criminal out of me.
Now they shall suffer the consequences
For I am not guilty.

No one ruin my dreams in vain
And lives his own dreams.
Authority or no authority.
Somebody's going to pay.
I shall start with these horny faggots
Who keep harassing me in the shower.

From now on I will pick up my soap.
And I dare anyone to even budge my way
For I shall relieve him off his sexual tension.
I carry a sharp blade
And I was brought in here a virgin
So I will not break out of here molested.

I have no right to be here
For I've yet to commit a crime.
I have no right to be here
For I had no clue my friend had drugs in his car.
If no lawyer can get me out of here
I will check my way back out one way or another.

49

Mike Stevenson Fleury

THE LONG STARE

Every family has one.
It feeds people with all kinds of information.
It keeps kids busy.
It also keeps the entire world entertained.
It raises the kids.
It tells people how to live their lives.
It doesn't distinguish.
It releases good information and bad information.
It doesn't care.
Doesn't care if the bad information falls in the wrong hands.
Every family has one.
No harm is ever intended,
But it's always how people use its information.
So as long as people have sight
As long as there's television
The long stare is on to last.

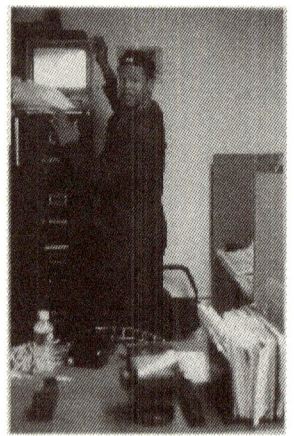

THE NIGHTMARE

I fell asleep finding myself in a peculiar place.
In sight stood a dreadful shadow
Attempting to chase me.
Covered in dust
I rain into the woods.
Almost suddenly
Daylight flipped into moonlight.
I looked in the sky
The sun was no longer there.
It was replaced by a huge red moon.
A moon, with a mind of its own.
The shadow kept pursuing me deeper into the woods.
Lost in the dark
The angry red moon started glaring at me.
Although frightened and helpless
I kept running for an escape.
Instead I found myself
Continuously falling
Into a bottomless hole.

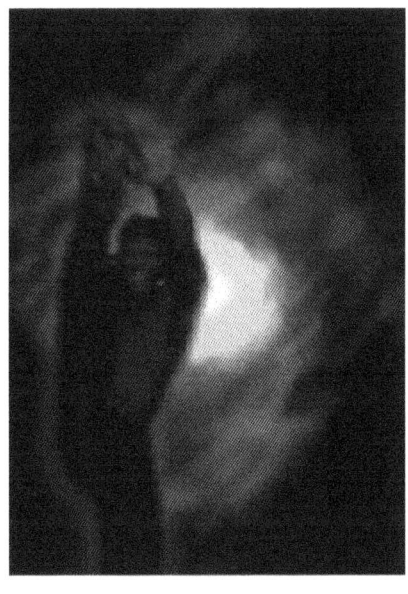

Mike Stevenson Fleury

THE FREE SPIRITS

Cruising through the air,
Lke butterflies,
My love and I head for everlasting peace.
Heart to heart,
We're both cuddling
With bodies coupling together.
Soul to soul,
We cut through the wind effortlessly.
Free at last,
We are being carried with no interference
Away from all pain and struggle
By the power of love.
With the engine of our heart,
And the sweat of our bodies
We cruise to happiness.
They keep us cruising peacefully,
Freely,
Far away,
Forever.

HEART OF VENGEANCE

The day I got the bad news
Was the day I became a killer.
His name was Patrick.
He was my friend.
A true friend.
Died by a jealous friend's bullet.
We graduated Junior High together.
We graduated High School together.
But we never attended the same college.
As a result he made some bad friends
And made some wrong choices.
His death had brought me many sleepless nights
And a few nightmares.
I thought avenging his death would bring me peace of mind.
I bought the gun
But my investigations took me nowhere.
Neither did the cops'.
The hoodlum had escaped to Haiti.
Patrick never liked partying,
But he was introduced to it.
Every time I see his fatherless son and singled girlfriend
I get overwhelmingly emotional.
Having had a pretty girlfriend and a nice car
Were the motive for the senseless death.
Nothing else had triggered the gunman's jealousy
To make him walk up to Patrick,
Point that gun to his head,
And pull that trigger.
One cheap bullet!
That's all it can take to lose a friend.
I know he's looking at me right this minute,
From high above,
Telling me to let go.
I'm so happy
For he is at a better place.
But I am sad
For the killer has gotten away.
I'm happy for having not witnessed the crime
For I would be sitting on death row right this minute.

BABY I DO BELIEVE

It's not the first time I've seen you
Although at times you make it seem
I sit alone on this lonely night
Thinking of what's really right
I say it seems hopeless to think of her
Since we can never be together
You may say there's no way in hell
But I'm here to tell you baby

(Chorus)
Baby, I do believe
That your heart desires me
Though it seems to me you don't realize
You know one's feelings never lie to him
Baby, please take my hand
So I could teach you right
Though it seems to me you are confused
You know one's feelings never lie to him

Now's the time to let me know
That I am really one true soul
You have to start being true inside
Or else you will keep us aside
I say there's no one out there, baby
Who can bring you much more joy
The right one's right here, baby
So I beg you open your heart

(Chorus)

You've got to follow your heart
For it will never deceive you
I swear there's nothing to fear
Since I truly am your soul mate
I say this gentle heart is waiting
It will show you heaven
A place where we can make love
So you've got to trust me, my love

(Chorus)

(Bridge)
Oh baby, do you think I'm wrong
If I am please slap me
Baby I see it in you
Oh I see you agree

It's not the first time I've seen you
But today you make me feel special
So come and give me that hug
I hate to see you waste your tears
I say baby there's no need to cry
I sure am glad you have discovered
I say that we belong together   ***(Fade and repeat)***

55

THE PERFECT WIFE

The perfect wife is responsible and faithful.
She surprises her husband in her sexy lingerie.
She listens and avoids arguing.
She takes care of the house,
The cooking, the kids, and some bills.
She's romantic and has a sense of humor.
She treats her husband with respect and dignity.
She is very organized and proud of her husband.
She makes sure the children behave well in public
And in the house.
She doesn't overspend
And she keeps no secrets from her husband.

THE PERFECT HUSBAND

The perfect husband is responsible and faithful.
He surprises his wife with flowers and gifts.
He makes sure that his wife is happy at all times.
He offers her all kinds of support and comfort
When she's down.
He helps around the house
With the bills and the children.
He makes her feel special
And number one everyday.
He makes a good father figure.
And he protects his house
And the family.

THE PERFECT DAUGHTER

The perfect daughter has morals.
She's religious
And brings home no immoral guys.
She believes in no teen sex.
She believes in no sex before marriage.
Therefore, she has no children.
She's a bright student.
She chooses her friends cautiously.
She is smart and obeys her parents.
She has common sense
And does no drugs.
She has many goals and dreams.
Therefore, doesn't get influenced.
And she stays out of trouble.

THE PERFECT MOTHER

The perfect mother comes with great responsibilities.
She raises her children with morals.
She never behaves improperly before her kids.
She takes good care of her children.
She doesn't smoke, drink, do drugs, nor go to clubs,
For kids are tape recorders.
Monkey see, monkey do!

Mike Stevenson Fleury

THE PERFECT SON

I'm the perfect son.
I respect and obey my parents.
I do not smoke and drink
Nor do I do any drugs.
I avoid the bad crowds
So I don't get in trouble.
I'm very smart and talented
And I get good grades.
I like girls but I want to save myself for marriage.

IMPERFECTION

When we think of America
We think of it as the greatest country.
Yet a lot of bad things still occur here.
So what really makes a country the greatest?
Is it injustice or lazy leaders?
Is it gun violence or drug abusers?
How about too many prisons?
How long will it take to try other methods?
How about an eye for an eye
Instead of free motels?
Which makes me wonder
Why am I working so hard
To only have my tax money wasted?
Maybe I should go take care of some cops
And let the state take care of me for a change?
Stupid idea you might say?
But who's really the stupid one here?
Free lunch, free cable, and free library.
Free weight room and free education.
Can you think of a better retirement?
Why wouldn't criminals envy so-called prison?
We have repeat offenders because they have it easy
And being away from society is not punishment.
Why not dump them in some Latin American jungle?
The tigers, the lions, or other beasts
Would show them a real punishment.
I believe in canning every week,
And strict rehabilitation.
Or the criminals will always win
For they laugh at our faces
While their victims keep on losing.

61

BABY LOVE

I was still in Junior High School
When I became pregnant.
I had to keep it a secret
Or my parents would kill me.
I was so embarrassed
And wanted to abort it.
I could not
For all the clinics would tell
my parents.
I just wanted it out of me fast.
So I tried to kill my baby.
I did all kinds of drugs with
my friends.
It was still moving inside me.
Today I still see in the news
Young girls killing and abandon their enfants.
So like them I never wanted a baby.
I just wanted to be a kid again.
So I made a mistake getting myself pregnant
I was too young to be a mother.
So when water started pouring out of me
I knew I had to leave school in a flash.
Safe out of my home's bathroom
I painfully got it out of me.
Tried to flush it down the toilet
But it would not go down.
I thought of chopping it up first
But I was already surrounded and covered with blood.
So I cautiously open the window
And did the terrible act.
I was never late for my next class
And no one ever found out who did it.
No one knew I was pregnant
And no one knew I left school.
You might call it evil
But I saw the baby as a nuisance.
It was a matter of life and death.
It was either me or the baby.
So naturally, I chose to be a kid again.
And now I'm free and a kid again.

OUTLAW

I'm an outlaw
And I'm damn proud of it.
I was born to live,
So I live my life in disguise.
I'm a good guy in the day
But I'm a misfit at night.
I walk in and out of jail.
I use the system
For I am still a minor
In the law's eyes.
Can't be held for long in jail
For I'm still 17.
Adults don't have it easy.
I do.
They get punished to the fullest of the law.
But I still got a whole year to be bad.

THE POOR EXCUSE

She's a poor excuse for a mother.
She lives off welfare checks.
She raises her kids with no morals nor dignity
For she has none.
She brings different men to her apartment.
She's proud, clumsy, and lazy.
She's never worked in her life.
She smokes weed in the house.
She has threesomes
In front of the kids.
She curses her boyfriends
In front of the kids.
She curses the kids
In front of her boyfriends.
She lets her kids curse
In public.
The four-year-old boy
Is still in diapers.
She doesn't cook nor clean.
She and the kids eat Chinese food everyday.
At times she even forgets to flush.

ROAD RAGE

I'm an aggressive driver.
I will not allow people cutting me off.
I'll kill one for that.
I do not allow people driving slow in front of me.
I'll kill one for that.
I hate stupid drivers.
I'll kill one for that.
Oh no he didn't!
I know that ol' man didn't just cut me off!
Oh it's on now!
He's going down for that.
What's that shiny thing he's pointing at me?
Oh no, it's a gun!
And he's firing at me.
Oh no he's so dead!
Okay ol' man, you wanna play?
I'll play!
There, that should teach you.
See you in hell ol' man!
I hope you can fly.
But don't hit the water too hard.
Now who's next?
Hey you there!
What are you looking at?
You wanna a peace of this?
Oh no he didn't!
I know he didn't just give me the middle finger!
Oh yeah it's on!
He must be stupid
Thinking he can outrun my car.

PUNISHMENT

What a virus!
It fears nothing but itself.
It attacks everybody.
It does not discriminate.
Whoever looks for it gets it.
Young or old.
Male or female.
All you have to be is negligent,
And you shall have your death sentence.
The disease was sent down to us for a reason.
To control our sexual behaviors,
To clean up our dirty acts,
And to regulate overpopulation.
Do we deserve such punishment?
Probably not.
Do we need to control our hormones and dirty acts?
Definitely!
Unlike the government
God watches over everybody.
And he always puts his foot down
For he cares about his planet
And the way we live on it.

GRANDMA

I miss my grandma.
The only one who understood me.
The only one who believed in me.
Now that I've made it big
I wanted to compensate her.
But now she's no longer here
I wish she were here.
I wish I had made it big earlier
For I would celebrate with her.

Mike Stevenson Fleury

THE BUS DRIVER

I'm a professional driver.
I drive a big bus,
I'm responsible for up to 55 lives everyday.
From kids to adults,
The mentally challenged and the disabled.
They all depend on me
For I hold their lives in my hands.
I'm so proud of my job
For I play a major role in the public transportation service.
I drive when it rains,
And I drive when it snows.
I am a professional driver.
And I show my professionalism
By giving the public a safe comfortable trip everyday.

THE FEAR

I'm not getting married
For it will be a waste of time.
I'm not getting married
For I don't want to be divorced.
I'm not getting married
For she will change.
I'm not getting married
For it'll be a one-day happiness.
I'm not getting married
For I will be homeless.
I'm not getting married
For she'll get fat and lazy.

STAND TALL

I used to stand tall
Now I sit low.
I used to run
Now I can't even walk
For I have a bullet in my back.
I used to be independent
Now my life has changed.
Give me back my legs!
I want back my mobility.
I used to leave footprints behind
But now I leave tire marks.
So life is nothing but a lease.

ENOUGH IS ENOUGH

I shall leave
For she uses me too much.
I shall leave
For she argues too much.
I shall leave
For she cheats too much.
I shall leave
For all my feelings for her are now gone.
I shall leave
For she won't know what she had till I'm gone.

ON AND OFF

I'm shutting off my brain
For I am tired of writing.
I'm shutting off my brain
For I am tired of thinking.
I'm shutting off my brain
For I am tired of concentrating
I'm shutting off my brain
For I am tired of observing.
I'm shutting off my brain
For I am tired of learning.
So I'm shutting off my brain.

A SILENT CRY

Wrapped in a belly
Desperate to come out
I wanted to see my new world
Which God and my parents had promised me.
I did not deserve a dead sentence
For I never did anything wrong.
I did not deserve a death sentence
For I was intended to be born.
Not to be destroyed before my time.
My crushed bones do not belong in a jar,
Nor a filthy trash can.
For I am not trash.
I needed to be born
For it was their intention
And my birth rights.
Although no one could hear my cry in the belly.
I was human.
I could feel.
I had many goals.
I could have been anything.
I could even be the one saving the world
From all sorts of invaders.
Why was I cheated of my existence.
Why mother?
How come you changed your mind?
Did you not want me in your world?
Did you not plan my existence?
Why was it so short?
Was it because you could not see me eye to eye?
Or perhaps the whole thing was to tease me?
You can't do that mother.
You just can't!
For I was once a small human.

Mike Stevenson Fleury

THE FORMER CITIZEN

I was born in a country called America.
I was a normal human citizen
But now I'm a former citizen
For I'm no longer human but an alien.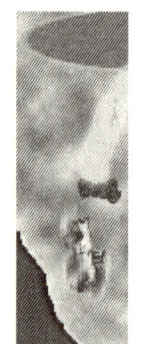
Aliens had rescued me two years ago
From the hands of a hate group.
They bombed my pickup truck with my family in it.
Following my family on my motorcycle
Out of that racist community
Almost got me killed too
But I was zapped off my bike right into an alien ship
Before my bike would follow my family
Off the big cliff.
The racists thought they had murdered me too
But they're in for a big surprise.
Now two years later
I'm a new individual, owned, biologically reprogrammed,
And partly controlled by the aliens.
Not from above,
But from their vessel located deep in the sea.
I'm here for two things.
Destroy all enemies and reprogram all that can be saved.
With this gun I can beam hatred out of people
And destroy all things that stand in the way.
When I'm being attacked by too many forces
I get some help from my alien friends.
My new bike is really out of this world
For it communicates with me in languages
Only I can understand.
It feeds me information and new assignments
Straight from the deep sea
Where a 24-hour worldwide surveillance is kept.
My new bike flies, floats, changes shapes
Complying to my rescues.
We won't leave this planet till I've completed this mission.
We will change the entire world one country at a time.
But we shall start with my former home, America.

THE TRANSFORMATION

The world is made of people and creatures.
Creatures treat other creatures equally
For creatures have no purpose for money nor fame.
I see many animals living together equally
For they have no money nor fame.
Money is evil
For it causes pain, blindness, and transgression.
Money is evil
For I've seen the transformation.
I see ugly people with money
Suddenly, are the prettiest.
I see the fattest people with money
Suddenly, are the skinniest.
I see criminals with money
Suddenly, are the friendliest.
I see stupid people with money
Suddenly, turned to be the smartest.
With money
The rich will always get respect.
Since money
Is the cause of their transformation
I guess the rich will always be on top
For they always look for ways to make more money.
As a result, old friends become
Invisible.
And the poor people become
Invisible,
As well as pests.

Mike Stevenson Fleury

TRAPPED IN A MIRROR

It all started with a long stare
Coming from a beauty
From across my apartment.
I was frozen.
Could not do anything but staring back.
Which one of us was the rude one?
I first ask myself.
But there was no rudeness at all.
She was simply speaking to me.
Only, not verbally.
I took a step forward
And so did she.
I took another step
But she took two
And the rest was history.
Suddenly I was blown away backward
With her arms tightly wrapped around my neck
As I was being seduced with a long sensual kiss,
Pushing me back into my apartment.
I could still see the mirrors in her eyes
Where I noticed my reflection trembling
As it asked for more.
Scary to know that she could hear every word I thought of.
I wouldn't even dare think of the word enough
For she would hear it.
Then the infatuation had turned into a dreadful night
For she would not leave
Nor speak a word.
Oh she scared me!
If ghosts had flesh and bones
I'd say she was one of those sexy quiet ones.
But I could not refuse her obsession
For I had a thirst for her unusual seduction.

I GOT HOOKED

It was on a Sunday morning
I felt like going to fish
When I saw that lovely girl
Staring at my face
Since I've seen that look before
I did know what she meant
So I rode my motorcycle
Headed right to her

(Chorus)
Oh I got hooked
Like a bird in a cage
Like a fish on a hook
That are willing to get caught
Oh I got hooked
Like a bird in a cage
Like a fish on a hook
That are willing to get caught

It was on that same Sunday
She asked me to give her a call
So we can go see the town
And wear my best suit
For I am a rich boy
I do like dressing in suits
When I go to the town
Looking for a date

(Chorus)

I can't wait until she's mine
Cause I know how to treat her
For it is not every day
One gets so lucky
Oh I feel so fortunate
For that Sunday morning
Having met that wonderful girl
Has brought me so much joy

(Chorus)

Mike Stevenson Fleury

THE WATCHER'S WATCHER

I watch him every night
Watching her jog
In her sweat and skimpy outfit.
I observe him watching her every move.
Every step that she takes,
And every deep breath she takes passing by.
He watches her as she sheds off the pounds
Every night in the park
Awaiting till she drops to the right size,
The right shape,
The right weight,
Before making his move.
Easy prey or stupid prey?
Jogging so late every night.
For when he attacks,
Violating every part of her,
Taking with him her dignity
And former admiration for men.
Who's to blame?
Who or what triggered the assault,
Such unspeakable act,
And unwanted pregnancy?
Is it the rapist or the victim?
Well my answer is exactly what you're thinking.

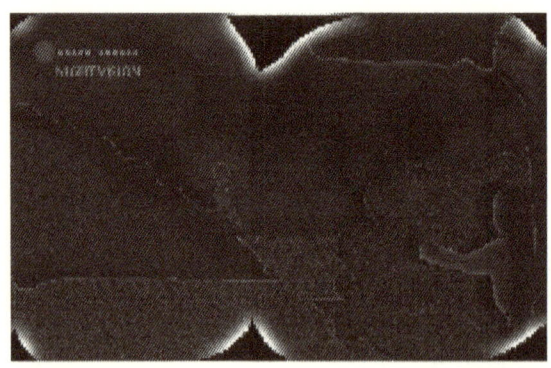

HOUSE OF HELL

I've seen that house.
I've been there many times.
My presence was never respected.
I was nothing but just another boyfriend.
I could not embarrass girlfriend.
I stayed a bit longer
For I had to learn as much as I could.
To them everything was normal.
All the fighting,
Cursing,
Arguing,
And screaming.
Yes, the screaming!
Their ways of communicating.
But I could never hear myself think.
I could not intervene
For they would not hear a word
Coming out of my mouth.
I wanted peace and out,
But could not embarrass girlfriend
For I really love her.

Mike Stevenson Fleury

THE ELDERLY

Oh the elderly!
A record of history.
A library of the past.
Oh I love history!
Old people, old news.
If only I could open their minds
And explore their preserved library.
If only for a short time I could relive
The past through them
I'd love them even more.
Still I've great respect for them
For they are rare and special.
Still I've great respect for them
For they give great advice.
Still I listen to them
For they know best.
Their gentleness and fragile nature
Are still quite fascinating to me.

CATCH THAT CHICKEN

I was driving down the road
When a chicken flew out of its moving trailer.
Out of hundreds
Only one lousy chicken worked out an escape plan.
And I was so hungry
For I had been driving for days.
Being short of cash
That chicken was a lifesaver.
So I had to do it.
I stepped on the gas
Hitting it with my windshield.
How mean of me one might say.
But it was a free chicken.
Free food from heaven.
All I had to do was to catch that chicken.
So the foot chase was on.
I was out of breath
But it could not fly any higher
For I hit very hard.
I remember devouring some chicken
As I walk back to my truck.
Still I can't recall ever cooking that chicken.
Perhaps it was the caveman in me acting up again.

Mike Stevenson Fleury

HOLD ON

Girl, hold on to your man
For there are hungry eyes watching.
Man, hold on to your girl
For there are hungry eyes watching.
Girlfriends can be obtained
But the challenge is keeping them
Boyfriends can be obtained
But the challenge is keeping them
Keeping a partner happens only if
The couple follows the rules
For it takes money and tolerance,
Forgiveness and unselfishness,
True love and understanding,
Sexual fulfilment and faithfulness
Meaning that,
Your partner is the one.
The only one.
So girl, hold on to your man
For there are some hungry eyes watching.
And man, hold on to your girl
For there are some hungry eyes watching.

DEATH

I welcome death
Only if it is invited.
An uninvited death
Will never be invited
For I value my life too much
To allow it to be taken from me.
I value my life too much
For it is the most valuable thing to me.
I will not let it be taken away
For I will defend it in ever way.
Challenge me with a bullet
You shall go down first.
Challenge me with a lancet
You shall bleed first.

Mike Stevenson Fleury

TAKE ME OUT OF THE JAR

I'm a hard working driver.
Everyone wants a piece of me.
The discreditable judges,
The lying cops,
And the money-hungry uncle Sam.
I keep watching him take big trunks out of my paychecks
There's nothing I can do.
I've seen the crooked judges finding innocent drivers guilty.
There's nothing we can do.
We could stop driving
For the bucks would stop there.
As it would mean no more false charges
And no more biting off our checks.
But we'd also lose
For we've got bills to pay and families to take care of.
We cannot be forced to criminal lifestyles
We have our reputation to protect.
But there's no way around their system.
It's either you live or die.
It's either you're in or out.
As long as I keep driving
I'll always find myself in their big jar
Filled with water,
Where they keep dumping
Their flesh-eating sharks
To pursue and annoy me
Until I give up in life,
Collapse, and die.
But when I do run upon a shark again
Will be the day I'll call it quit
For I will do more than say my piece.

TRUE TEMPTATION

So I went and got myself a girlfriend.
For that reason
I feel I'm being tested
Everyday of my life.
And it's hard.
It's killing me.
So much pressure.
So much confusion.
I keep seeing
Gorgeous and sexy girls
Everywhere I turn.
I've got a girlfriend,
I say.
She's home.
I'm taken,
I keep repeating to myself.
But the seductions keep getting worse.
The girls seduce me up close
And the seduce me from a distance.
My body tells me to go for it,
But my heart tells me to keep walking.
What is this really
I'm confronted with?
What is it really
That's holding me back?
Could it really be
Love?
It should be
For I don't think with my body.
So I'm following my heart
For I cannot imagine my world
Without my girlfriend in it?

POLITICIANS

What a bowl of crock!
What lawyers!
What liars!
They are promise makers
But never promise keepers.
What actors!
Let the best liar
Be elected.
Let the best speech maker
Be elected.
What manipulators!
Let us be
manipulated
For we keep believing.
We should not be asked
To read their lips.
Instead they should read ours
For we the people should mean business.
We the people should be the ones
In control.
We should tell them
To keep making promises
For they'll be forced to keep them
Or they shall be jailed for lying to the people,
Lying to be elected.
I promise that way
We'll have honest leaders,
An honest society,
And an honest country
For we the people
Will never be lied to ever again.

IT'S TIME

The plan had failed long ago.
We do not deserve any more chances.
Let the comets come down!
For I am ready to check out.
I have seen enough.
Too much evil on this planet.
We have failed the test terribly.
Too much greed and racism.
No peace nor harmony
For evil has corrupted our minds.
There's no hope now.
Let the comets come down!
Right this minute
Before we bomb every country to the sea.
Right this minute
Before we destroy nature.
Let them come now
For every country has a big bomb
Pointed at each other.
Let them come now
For I have made peace with God.
Let them come now
For I've accomplished the purpose of my existence.
And let them come now
For I refuse to die in the hands of evil.

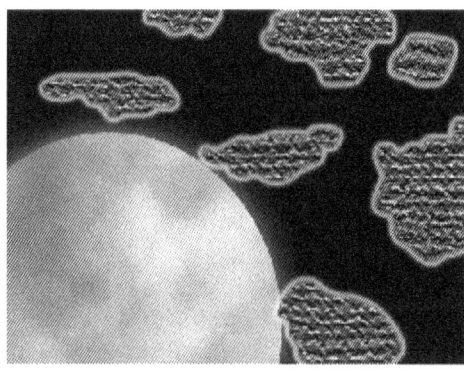

Mike Stevenson Fleury